MOTOCROSS

Frances Ridley

Editorial Consultant – Cliff Moon

nasen
NASEN House, 4/5 Amber Business Village, Amber Close,
Amington, Tamworth, Staffordshire B77 4RP

Rising Stars UK Ltd.
22 Grafton Street, London W1S 4EX
www.risingstars-uk.com

Every effort has been made to trace copyright holders and
obtain their permission for use of copyright material. The
publisher will gladly receive information enabling them to
rectify any error or omission in subsequent editions.
All facts are correct at time of going to press.

Text © Rising Stars UK Ltd.
The right of Frances Ridley to be identified as the author
of this work has been asserted by her in accordance with
the Copyright, Design and Patents Act, 1988.

Published 2006

Cover design: Button plc
Cover image: Buzz Pictures/Alamy
Illustrator: Bill Greenhead
Technical Adviser: Steve Dale
Text design and typesetting: Nicholas Garner, Codesign
Educational consultants: Cliff Moon and Lorraine Petersen
Pictures: Alamy; pages 5, 12, 13, 16, 18, 20, 24, 36, 37:
Buzz Pictures; pages 6, 8, 11, 28, 29, 37: Getty Images;
pages 4, 21, 25, 28, 37: raychuss.com; 8, 9, 29, 32, 43

This book should not
be used as a guide to
the sports shown in it.
The publishers accept
no responsibility for
any harm which might
result from taking
part in these sports.

All rights reserved. No part of this publication may be
reproduced, stored in a retrieval system, or transmitted in
any form by any means, electronic, mechanical,
photocopying, recording or otherwise without the prior
permission of Rising Stars UK Ltd.

British Library Cataloguing in Publication Data.
A CIP record for this book is available from the British
Library.

ISBN: 1-905056-97-4
Printed by Craft Print International Ltd, Singapore

Contents

What is motocross?

Motocross is a kind of motorbike racing.

Motocross tracks are outdoors.

Riders go up steep hills and down steep drops.

They jump off ramps and go round corners.

Motocross facts

Scrambling is the old name for motocross.

MX is the short name for motocross.

A motocross race is called a moto.

Motocross bikes

Motocross bikes are not like other motorbikes.

They go up hills and over jumps – so they need good **acceleration**.

Seat

Exhaust

They have to go on mud, sand and dirt – so they need tyres with good grip.

Safety Tip!

Keep your bike in good working order.

They have to land after jumps – so they need good **suspension**.

Engine

Gears

Brakes

Motocross kit

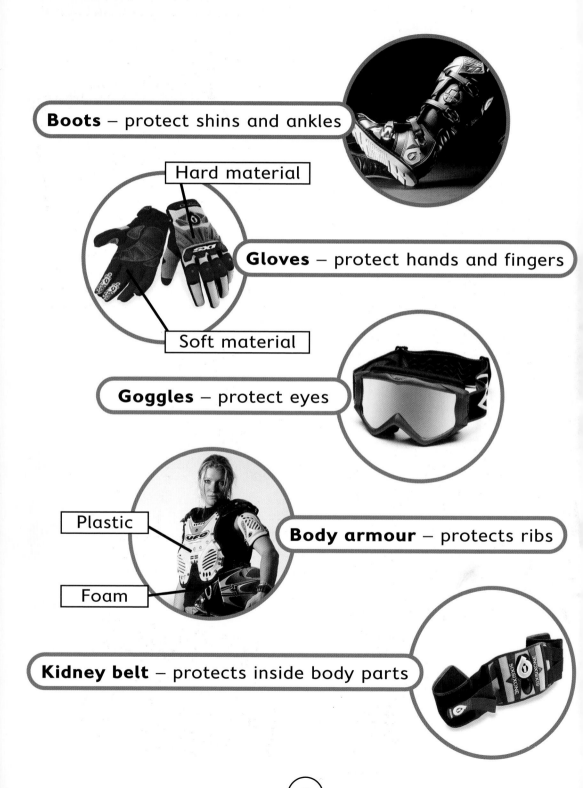

Boots – protect shins and ankles

Hard material

Gloves – protect hands and fingers

Soft material

Goggles – protect eyes

Plastic

Body armour – protects ribs

Foam

Kidney belt – protects inside body parts

Clothing – protects body, arms and legs

Tips!

✗ Never buy a second-hand helmet.

✓ Make sure your helmet fits well.

Helmet – protects head

Safety Tip!

Always wear the right kit.

Pads – protect knees

Tip!

New boots are stiff – wear them in before you ride.

Get into motocross

Get started

Go to a track school.

Borrow a bike and kit.

Get serious

Ride at a practice track.

Buy a bike and kit.

Get racing!

Find a motocross club near you.

Enter an event.

Motocross clubs

There are lots of local motocross clubs.

They run races from March to October.

Most races are at weekends.

Think about these things before you join a motocross club.

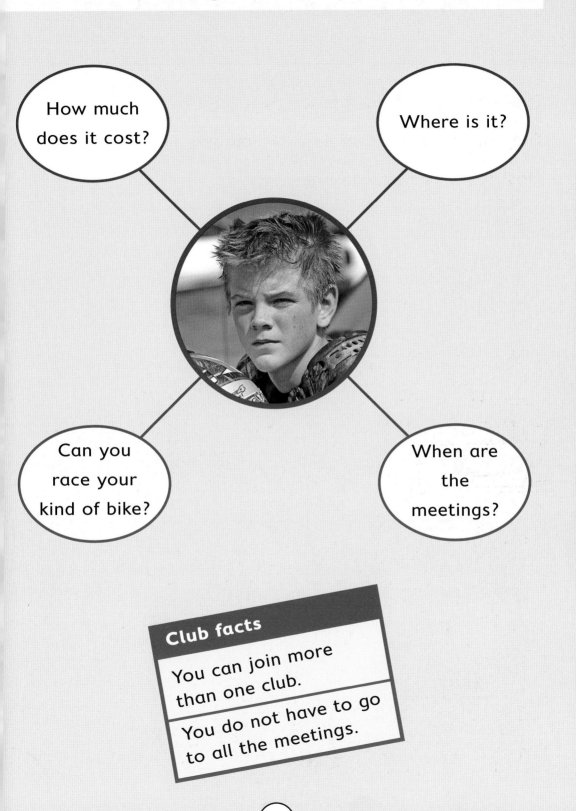

How much does it cost?

Where is it?

Can you race your kind of bike?

When are the meetings?

Club facts

You can join more than one club.

You do not have to go to all the meetings.

Motocross people

Most people working at motocross clubs are not paid.

They love motocross and they help for free.

Clerk of course

- Makes sure the track is safe.

- Makes sure the riders follow the rules.

Scrutineer

Makes sure the bikes and kit are safe.

Starter

Starts all the races.

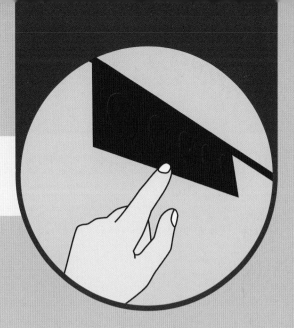

Track marshal

- Stands by the track when a race is on.

- Gives riders flag signals.

- Helps riders if they get hurt.

Lap scorer

Keeps score of the points.

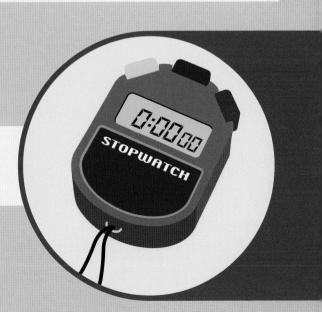

Race information

Classes

Motocross riders race in different classes.

Class	Age	Engine size
Junior	6 – 10 years	Max 65cc
Intermediate	9 – 12 years	Max 85cc
Senior	11 – 15 years	Max 100cc
Open	14 – 17 years	Max 125cc

Races

There are forty riders in each race.

You do two or three races at an event.

Points

You get points for each race.
Your points are added together.

The winner is the rider with the most points.

Flags

Track marshals use flags to give warnings to the riders.

All riders must stop

 This rider must stop now

 Great danger – slow down and stop

 Track is clear

 Let rider behind pass by

 Rider needs first aid

Last lap

Finish

Starting and finishing a race

The race starts when the **start gate** drops.

① The starter points to the red **lights**.

② The starter runs off the track.

③ The riders start when the lights go out.

Start gate

The winner is the first rider to finish the last lap.

(1) The winner crosses the finish line.

(2) A track marshal starts waving a flag.

(3) The other riders cross the finish line.

(4) The marshal stops waving the flag.

Race day

There are lots of things to do before the race starts.

Scrutineering

Go to the **scrutineer**.

The scrutineer checks you are safe to race.

Race control

Sign in at the desk.

Get your race number.

Check the race order.

Practice sessions

Go to the practice session.

Do three laps of the track.

Race day 2

Your race is about to start – but you still have things to do!

Go to the **collecting area** and get your **grid** number.

Go to **grid** position and do a warm-up lap.

Return to your grid position.

Look at the starter and look at the **lights**.

Rev your bike and go!

Motocross tracks

There are motocross tracks all over the country and every track is different.

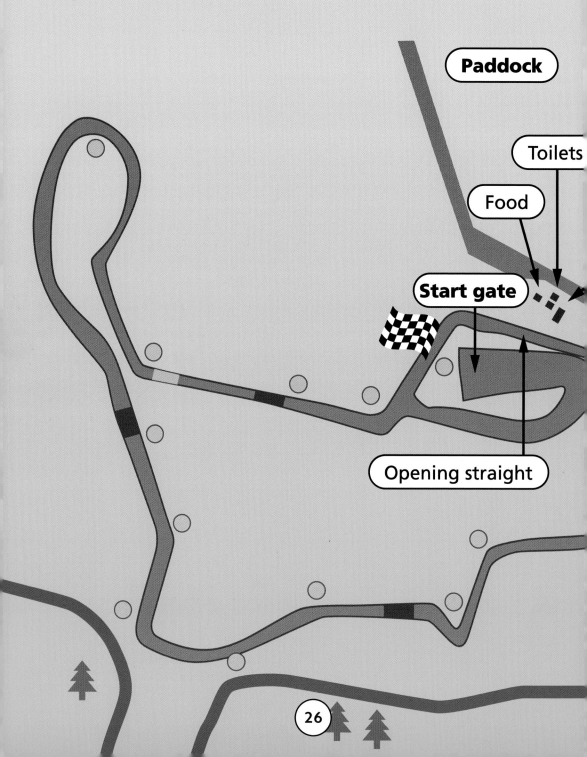

Paddock

Toilets

Food

Start gate

Opening straight

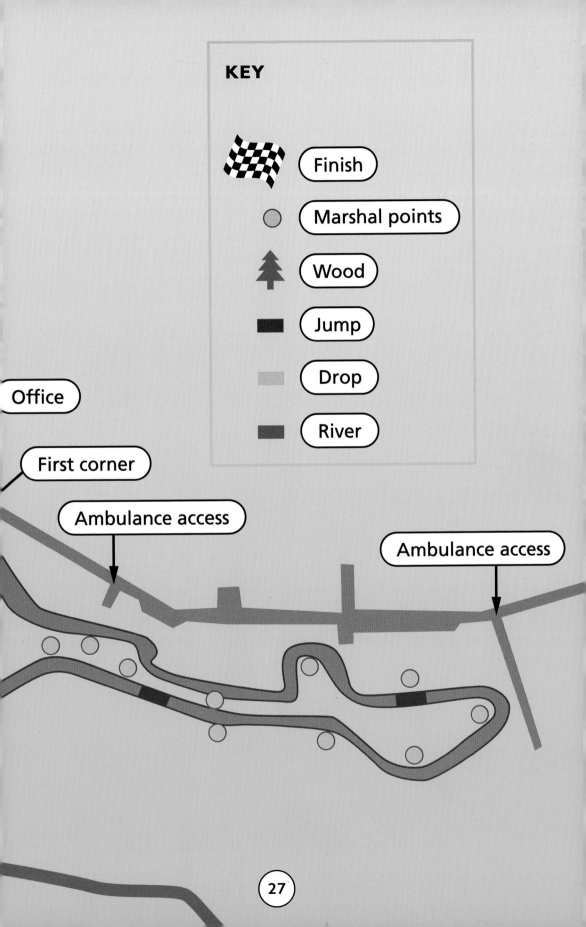

KEY

Finish

Marshal points

Wood

Jump

Drop

River

Office

First corner

Ambulance access

Ambulance access

On the track

Most tracks have corners, jumps, drops and obstacles.

Corners

Slow down before you get to the corner.

Lean into the corner as you go round it.

Jumps

Get faster as you go up the jump.

Land on your back wheel.

Drop-offs

Drop-offs are steep drops in the track.

Land on both wheels.

Obstacles

Obstacles are things in your way.

Don't look at the obstacle – look for a way round it!

Tip!

Don't look right in front of the bike. Look ahead.

Safety tips!

Don't show off.

Move your bike off the track if it stops.

Don't cross in front of other riders.

Ben's Story (Part one)

Hi, I'm Ben and I love motocross.

Dad showed me how to ride. We went to the track every weekend. Mum came too. It was fun.

Last year, everything changed.

Dad was riding at the track. He lost control of his bike. He fell off and broke his neck.

He died before the ambulance got to him.

SHOCK MOTOCROSS DEATH

'Wheelie' Wilson dies at track.

The motocross club lost its best rider on Saturday. Pete Wilson fell off his bike and broke his neck.

This year has been hard. I miss Dad.

I still love motocross. I still go to the track every week. But Mum won't come with me. She won't have anything to do with motocross.

I miss Mum, too.

Continued on page 34

Junior champions

There are championships at four levels — Club, Regional, National and International.

There are three national junior championships — BYMX 125cc, BSMA 125cc and KWS 125cc.

Championship fact!

Ray Rowson won all three championships in 2004. He was 16 years old.

The FIM Junior World Championship has two classes.

80cc class — 12 years or older

125cc class — 15 years or older

Can I be a junior champion?

You need help

You have to be good

You have to practise

You need **coaching**

You need **sponsorship**

Ben's Story (Part two)

I'm a good motocross rider. I want to be a
champion – but I need help!

Mum won't help me. She won't drive the van.
She won't pay for a bigger bike.
She won't pay for coaching.

She wants me to stop motocross. She says it
costs too much.

We have rows about it.

"You're scared!" I shout. "You're scared that
 I'll die too!"

"That is not fair, Ben!"

I need help.

I send an email to Tod Black. Tod Black is a top motocross rider.

It's the championship on Saturday.

Tod has to see me race! He'll see how good I am. He will want to help me.

Continued on page 38

The ACU Academy

The ACU Academy started in 2000.

It is for the best young motorbike riders.

The Academy gives riders **coaching** and help.

Kieran Clarke went to the ACU Academy.

He started motocross when he was seven.

Now he rides superbikes.

Kieran Clarke

You learn about lots of different things at the Academy.

Riding skills

Media

Diet

Fitness

Race tactics

Sponsorship

Academy facts

| The Academy takes 13- to 17-year-olds. |
| You go to the Academy for three years. |
| You do not have to pay. |

37

Ben's Story (Part three)

I go to the Championship on my bike.

No van. No Mum. No Tod.

I'm on my own.

I make a bad start in the first race. Josh is in front of me. Then he falls off his bike! I lose loads of places.

I get up to fourth place by the second lap.
I finish third.

It's good – but not that good. I wish that Mum
was here. I go back to the paddock. Someone
calls my name – it's Mum! She has come to the
race after all!

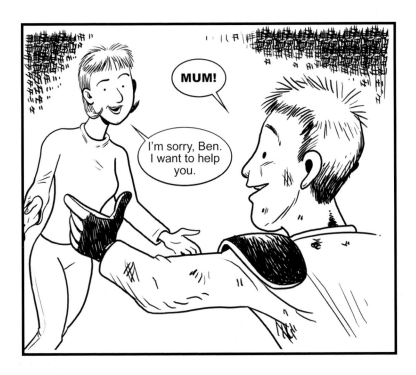

I make a good start in the second race. I'm
second round the corner. Then I lose out to
Tom. I finish in second place.

Josh and I are equal on points. It's down to the
third race now.

Continued on the next page

At the end of the second race Mum comes over. She has a man with her.

"Hi Ben," says the man. "I am Alex Biggs. Tod Black told me about you."

I nearly drop my helmet. Alex Biggs is a top motocross coach!

"I want to take you on," he says. "For free!"

"Great!" I shout.

I make a great start in the third race. But Josh wants to win, too! We are neck and neck in the third lap. It's fun! But there is no stopping me. Josh lets me by. I win the race. I am in overall first place.

I am the junior champion!

We go back to the van. Mum makes a cup of tea.

"That was a great race," says Mum. "Your dad would have been proud of you."

The Motocross of Nations

The Motocross of Nations is the 'Olympic Games of motocross'.

Each country enters a team of three riders.

The riders are in three different classes.

There are three rounds. The riders get points and the team with the most points wins.

Facts!

Motocross of Nations started in 1947.

30,000 people go to the event.

36 teams went to the 2005 Motocross of Nations.

The US team won 13 times in a row from 1981 to 1993.

Quiz

1. What is the old name for motocross?

2. What kind of tyres does a motocross bike have?

3. How do you choose a safe motocross helmet?

4. How many riders take part in a race?

5. Who checks that the bikes are safe?

6. Who starts the race?

7. How do you land after a drop-off?

8. Who won three junior national championships in 2004?

9. When did the ACU Academy start training riders?

10. How many teams were in the 2005 Motocross of Nations?

Glossary of terms

acceleration	Going faster – motocross bikes accelerate very fast.
armour	Hard pads on motocross clothes.
coaching	Teaching in sport.
collecting area	Where riders go before a race.
diet	The food you eat.
grid	Where riders line up to start the race.
lights	Two red lights go on before the race starts – the race starts when the lights go off.
media	Newspapers, magazines, radio, television.
paddock	Where riders go when they are not racing.
scrutineer	Checks that riders' bikes and kit are safe.
sponsorship	Gives riders bikes and kit for free – the bike and kit have the sponsor's name on.
start gate	Metal gate in front of bike at start line – it drops when the lights go out.
suspension	Part of bike – takes the shock out of hard landings.

More Resources

Books

Motocross, Gary Freeman, Radical Sports Series, Heinemann Library (ISBN 1-43103-699-3)
Tips on riding, looking after your bike and keeping safe.

Dirt Rider's Off-Road Riding Techniques, Motorbooks International (ISBN 0-76031-315-6)
Packed with great photos and lots of info.

Newspapers and Magazines

Trials and Motocross News
Johnstone Press New Media

MotoX Magazine
Motoplay Publications Ltd

Websites

www.rideoffroad.co.uk
A great site for basic tips.

www.bbc.co.uk/shropshire/content/articles/2005/08/30/sport_rowson_wins_bymx_feature.shtml
Info on Ray Rowson – with videos!

www.acu.org.uk/info/disciplines/motocross.aspx
The Auto Cycle Union's official site. Lots of info and tips.

DVDs

This is Motocross (Cat. no. DM2277)
How to get started in motocross – and how to get to the top!

Crash Kings (Cat. no. DM2501)
The title says it all!

Motovation – The Rick Johnson Technique (Cat. no. DM2158)
Tips on riding and looking after your bike.

Answers

1 Scrambling

2 Tyres with a good grip.

3 It fits well/It is not second-hand.

4 About 40.

5 The scrutineer.

6 The starter.

7 Land on both wheels.

8 Ray Rowson

9 2000

10 36

Index